Esther

Finding Yourself in Times of Trouble

Drawn in
BIBLE STUDY

Eugene H. Peterson

THE**MESSAGE**

NAVPRESS

A NavPress resource published in alliance with Tyndale House Publishers, Inc.

NavPress is the publishing ministry of The Navigators, an international Christian organization and leader in personal spiritual development. NavPress is committed to helping people grow spiritually and enjoy lives of meaning and hope through personal and group resources that are biblically rooted, culturally relevant, and highly practical.

For more information, visit www.NavPress.com.

Esther: Finding Yourself in Times of Trouble

Copyright © 2017 by Eugene H. Peterson. All rights reserved.

A NavPress resource published in alliance with Tyndale House Publishers, Inc.

NAVPRESS, the NAVPRESS logo, *THE MESSAGE*, and THE MESSAGE logo are registered trademarks of NavPress, The Navigators, Colorado Springs, CO. *TYNDALE* is a registered trademark of Tyndale House Publishers, Inc. Absence of ® in connection with marks of NavPress or other parties does not indicate an absence of registration of those marks.

The Team:
Don Pape, Publisher
David Zimmerman, Editor
Jennifer Ghionzoli, Designer

Cover and interior illustrations are the property of their respective copyright holders, and all rights are reserved. Cover illustration by Lizzie Preston © NavPress; cover watercolor texture © Charles Perrault/Adobe Stock. Interior borders and other images on pages 13, 26, 59, 64–66, and 71 © Felicity French/Advocate Inc.; interior geometric pattern © Vítek Prchal/Creative Market; all other interior illustrations by Lizzie Preston, Angelika Scudamore, and Jennifer Tucker © NavPress.

The author is represented by the literary agency of Alive Literary Agency, 7680 Goddard St., Suite 200, Colorado Springs, CO 80920, www.aliveliterary.com.

All Scripture quotations are taken from *THE MESSAGE*, copyright © 1993, 1994, 1995, 1996, 2000, 2001, 2002 by Eugene H. Peterson. Used by permission of NavPress. All rights reserved. Represented by Tyndale House Publishers, Inc.

Some content from the introduction and "How to Get the Most out of Esther" is adapted from *Eat This Book*, copyright © 2006 by Eugene H. Peterson. Published by Eerdmans. Reprinted by permission of the publisher; all rights reserved. Some content is adapted from *Five Smooth Stones for Pastoral Work*, copyright © 1992 by Eugene H. Peterson. Published by Eerdmans. Reprinted by permission of the publisher; all rights reserved. Some content from "How to Lead a Drawn In Bible Study" is adapted from Eugene H. Peterson, *The Wisdom of Each Other* (Grand Rapids, MI: Zondervan, 1998). The quotation from Tricia McCary Rhodes is from "Bible Study Meets Crafting," *Her.meneutics*, July 5, 2016, accessed July 8, 2016, at www.christianitytoday.com/women/2016/july/bible-study-meets-crafting-bible-journaling-craze.html?paging=off.

For information about special discounts for bulk purchases, please contact Tyndale House Publishers at csresponse@tyndale.com or call 800-323-9400.

ISBN 978-1-63146-787-5

Printed in China

23   22   21   20   19   18   17
7   6   5   4   3   2   1

contents

Introduction . . . *page v*

How to Get the Most out of Esther . . . page xi

page 1

— SESSION ONE —

This Is the Story of Something That Happened

ESTHER 1–2

page 21

— SESSION TWO —

If I Die, I Die

ESTHER 3–4

page 41

— SESSION THREE —

What Do You Want?

ESTHER 5–7

page 61

— SESSION FOUR —

How Can I Bear to Stand By?

ESTHER 8–10

How to Lead a Drawn In Bible Study . . . page 81

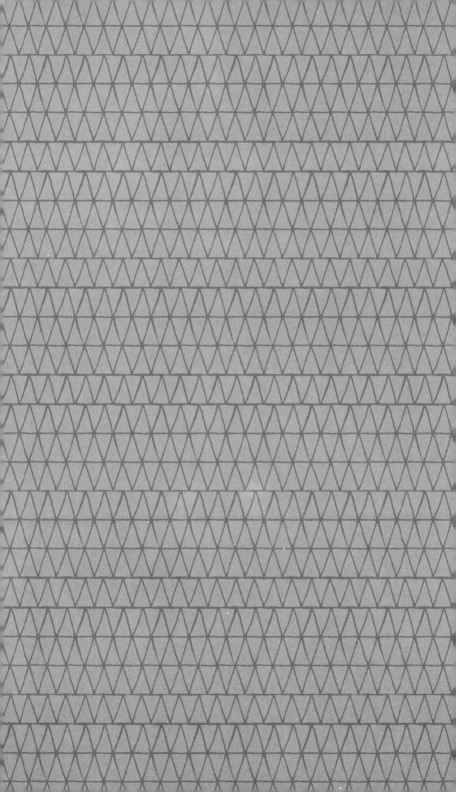

introduction

Eugene H. Peterson

READING IS THE FIRST thing, just reading the Bible. As we read, we enter a new world of words and find ourselves in on a conversation in which God has the first and last words. God uses words to form and bless us, to teach and guide us, to forgive and save us.

I didn't start out as a pastor. I began my vocational life as a teacher and for several years taught the biblical languages of Hebrew and Greek in a theological seminary. I expected to live the rest of my life as a professor and scholar, teaching and writing and studying. But then my life took a sudden vocational turn to pastoring a congregation.

I was now plunged into quite a different world. The first noticeable difference was that nobody seemed to care much about the Bible, which so recently people had been paying me to teach them. Many of the people I worked with now knew virtually nothing about it, had never read it, and weren't interested in learning. Many others had spent years reading it, but for them it had gone flat through familiarity, reduced to clichés. Bored, they dropped it. And there weren't many people in between. Very few were interested in what I considered my primary work, getting the words of the Bible into their heads and hearts, getting the message lived. They found newspapers and magazines, videos and pulp fiction more to their taste.

Meanwhile I had taken on as my life work the responsibility for getting these very people to listen—really listen—to the message in this book. I knew I had my work cut out for me.

I lived in two language worlds, the world of the Bible and the world of today. I had always assumed they were the same world. But these people didn't see it that way. So out of necessity I became a "translator" (although I wouldn't have called it that then), daily standing on the border between two worlds, getting the language of the Bible that God uses to create and save us, heal and bless us, judge and rule over us, into the language of today that we use to gossip and tell stories, give directions and do business, sing songs and talk to our children.

My intent is simply to get people reading the Bible who don't know that the Bible is readable at all, at least by them, and to get people who long ago lost interest in the

Bible to read it again. Read in order to live, praying as you read, "God, let it be with me just as you say."

INTRODUCTION TO ESTHER

The unknown Persian Jewish author of Esther probably lived sometime within 150 years of the events described in this story, while Persia was still in charge of the Middle East, before Alexander the Great took over. Jews under Persian rule refused to say that their God was only one among many options, and for that they endured social put-downs, job discrimination, and sometimes violence.

It seems odd that the awareness of God, or even of the people of God, brings out the worst in some people. God, the source of all goodness and blessing and joy, at times becomes the occasion for nearly unimaginable acts of cruelty, atrocity, and evil. There is a long history of killing men and women simply because they are perceived as reminders or representatives of the living God, as if killing people who worship God gets rid of God himself. To no one's surprise, God is still alive and present.

The book of Esther opens a window on this world of violence directed, whether openly or covertly, against God and God's people. The perspective it provides transcends the occasion that provoked it, a nasty scheme to massacre all the exiled Jews who lived in the vast expanse of fifth-century BC Persia.

Three characters shape the plot. Mordecai, identified simply as "the Jew," anchors the story. He is solid, faithful, sane, godly. His goodness is more than matched by the evil and arrogant vanity of Haman, who masterminds the planned massacre. Mordecai's young, orphaned, and ravishing cousin, Esther, whom he has raised, emerges from the shadows of the royal harem to take on the title role.

It turns out that no God-representing men and women get killed in this story—in a dramatic turnaround, the plot fails. But millions before and after Esther have been and, no doubt, will continue to be killed. There is hardly a culture or century that doesn't eventually find a Haman determined to rid the world of evidence and reminders of God. Meanwhile, Esther continues to speak the final and definitive word: *You can't eliminate God's people.* No matter how many of them you kill, you can't get rid of the communities of God-honoring, God-serving, God-worshiping people scattered all over the earth. This is still the final and definitive word.

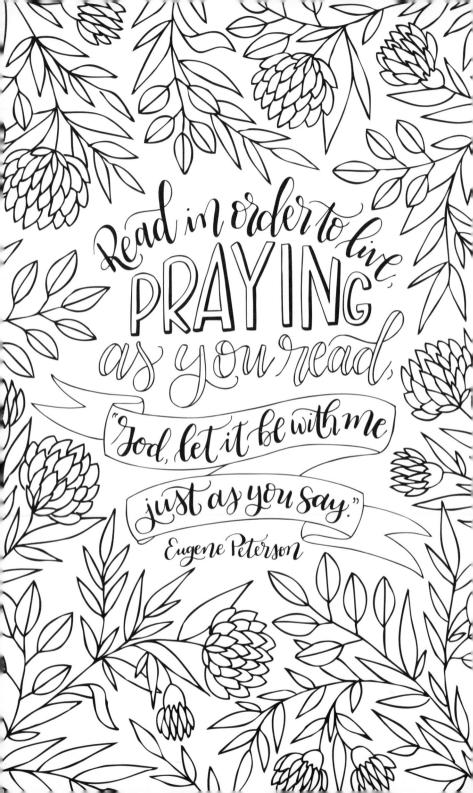

Read in order to live, PRAYING as you read, "God, let it be with me just as you say."

Eugene Peterson

It takes more than bread to stay alive.
It takes a steady stream of words from God's mouth.

MATTHEW 4:4

MANY PEOPLE APPROACH reading the Bible as a religious duty or a way to get in good with God. Worse still, some believe God will send a horrible punishment if they don't dedicate at least a half hour each day to dutiful study of his Word. Coming to the Bible with so much religious baggage takes all the fun out of reading it.

Reading the Bible isn't simply a fact-finding mission. You don't come just to collect bits of trivia about God. From the moment you read the first line of the Bible, you will discover that this book isn't about you. It's about God. God gave his Word as the place where you meet him face-to-face.

In order to read the Scriptures adequately and

accurately, it's necessary at the same time to live them—to live them *as* we read them. This kind of reading has been named by our ancestors as *lectio divina*, often translated "spiritual reading." It means not only reading the text but also meditating on the text, praying the text, and living the text. It is reading that enters our souls the way food enters our stomachs, spreads through our blood, and transforms us. Christians don't simply learn or study or use Scripture; we feed on it. Words spoken and listened to, written and read are intended to do something in us, to give us health and wholeness, vitality and holiness, wisdom and hope.

The Scriptures not only reveal everything of who God is but also everything of who we are. And this revelation is done in such a way as to invite participation on both sides, of author and reader.

This may be the single most important thing to know as we come to read and study and believe these Holy Scriptures: this rich, alive, personally revealing God as experienced in Father, Son, and Holy Spirit, personally addressing us in whatever circumstances we find ourselves, at whatever age we are, in whatever state we are. Christian reading is participatory reading, receiving the words in such a way that they become interior to our lives, the rhythms and images becoming practices of prayer, acts of obedience, ways of love. We submit our lives to this text so that God's will may be done on earth as it is in heaven.

One of the characteristic marks of the biblical story-tellers is a certain reticence. They don't tell us too much. They leave a lot of blanks in the narration, an implicit invitation to enter the story ourselves, just as we are, and to discover for ourselves how to fit in. There are, of course, always moral, theological, and historical elements in these stories that need to be studied, but never in dismissal of the story that is being told.

When we submit our lives to what we read in Scripture, we find that we're being led not to see God in our stories but to see our stories in God's. God is the larger context and plot in which our stories find themselves.

The Bible is God's Word. He spoke it into existence and he continues to speak through it as you read. He doesn't just share words on a page. He shares himself. As you meet God in this conversation, you won't just learn *about* him; you will *experience* him more deeply and more personally than you ever thought possible.

DRAWN IN BIBLE STUDIES

We all lead busy lives, and even when we step away from our activities for spiritual rest and renewal, our activities don't necessarily step away from us. *Drawn in* Bible Studies are designed to temporarily relieve you of distractions so you can enjoy the story of God more fully. This happens in a variety of ways:

The Coloring

For people of all ages, coloring offers a structured activity that fosters creative thinking. Tricia McCary Rhodes, author of *The Wired Soul*, is not surprised by the appeal of coloring among adults today:

> Brain scans of people involved in activities like coloring reveal that as we focus, our heart rate slows and our brain waves enter a more relaxed state. Over time, by engaging in Scripture or prayer art-journaling, it may become easier for us to focus and pay attention in other areas of our lives as well. It is no wonder we are so drawn to this activity.

As you work through a study, read the appropriate Bible passage and question, and mull over your response as you color. Some art has been provided for you, but feel free to draw in the open space as well. The act of coloring will help your "orienting response," the brain function that allows you to filter out background distractions and attend to the matter at hand. That's one reason so many people doodle as they read or study. Ironically, by coloring as you engage in this Bible study, you'll be more attentive to what the Scriptures have to teach you.

The Message

For many people, the Bible has become so familiar that it loses some of its resonance. They've memorized so many Scriptures, or heard so many sermons, that they think they've figured a passage out. For others, the Bible has never not been intimidating—its names and contexts separated from us by millennia, its story shrouded by memories of bad church experiences or negative impressions of people who claim it as their authority. While you can read any Bible translation you like alongside the *Drawn in* Bible Studies, included in the studies themselves are passages from *The Message*, a rendering of the Bible in contemporary language that matches the tone and informality of the original, ancient language. You will often be surprised by the way *The Message* translates something you may have read or heard many times before. And in that surprise, you'll be more receptive for what God might have for you today.

The Questions

When we sit down just to read the Bible, we can feel a bit disoriented. The questions in the *Drawn in* Bible Studies are designed to help you stay connected to your own lived experience even as you enter into the lived experience of the people and places the Scriptures introduce us to. You'll grow in your understanding of the Bible, but you'll also grow in your understanding of yourself. These questions are also good for discussion—get together with a group of friends, and enjoy coloring and talking together.

The Commentary

Included in this *Drawn in* Bible Study are occasional comments from renowned Bible teacher Eugene Peterson. You'll see his name following his comments. He helps clarify more confusing passages and offers insight into what's behind what you are reading. He'll help keep you from getting stuck.

Leader's Notes

In the section "How to Lead a *Drawn in* Bible Study" you'll find general guidelines for leading people through this study, along with notes specific to each session. These can inform and enhance your experience, so even if you are going through this study on your own, or if you are not the leader of a group discussion of this study, read through the notes as preparation for each session. Nevertheless, don't feel pressure to be an expert; the main purpose of this study is to provide an opportunity for fun and fellowship as people encounter God's Word and consider how it touches their lives.

This Is the Story of Something That Happened

ESTHER 1–2

SERVANTS GO ABOUT their work quietly and deferentially. They walk down the street and speak in soft conversational tones. They go about their work in gentleness. They don't stand over someone and bully. They stand under and serve.

To be a servant is to be like God, for God is in his creation serving it.

—EUGENE

1. Recall a time you worked as a "servant"—a job in a service industry, a voluntary role as a care provider, or some other "quiet" and "deferential" role. What was your experience like? What was good about it? What was hard about it?

2. Who are some of the people in your life who are "like God" in their servant attitude? What do you appreciate about them?

3. Even though "to be a servant is to be like God," very few people aspire to servanthood. Why is that?

*T*HIS IS THE story of something that happened in the time of Xerxes, the Xerxes who ruled from India to Ethiopia—127 provinces in all. King Xerxes ruled from his royal throne in the palace complex of Susa. In the third year of his reign he gave a banquet for all his officials and ministers. The military brass of Persia and Media were also there, along with the princes and governors of the provinces.

For six months he put on exhibit the huge wealth of his empire and its stunningly beautiful royal splendors. At the conclusion of the exhibit, the king threw a weeklong party for everyone living in Susa, the capital—important and unimportant alike. The party was in the garden courtyard of the king's summer house. The courtyard was elaborately decorated with white and blue cotton curtains tied with linen and purple cords to silver rings on marble columns. Silver and gold couches were arranged on a mosaic pavement of porphyry, marble, mother-of-pearl, and colored stones. Drinks were served in gold chalices, each chalice one-of-a-kind. The royal wine flowed freely—a generous king!

The guests could drink as much as they liked—king's orders!—with waiters at their elbows to refill the drinks. Meanwhile, Queen Vashti was throwing a separate party for women inside King Xerxes' royal palace.

ESTHER 1:1-9

4. *The Bible is mainly filled with stories about the Jews, God's chosen people, and their interactions with God. Yet the book of Esther begins with a story about a pagan king and an extravagant celebration. What expectations do you have for the rest of this book, given this unusual opening story?*

5. *Xerxes, described as "a generous king," throws "a weeklong party for everyone living in Susa, the capital—important and unimportant alike." What might be an equivalent event in contemporary society? Who might be an equivalent person to throw such an event?*

O N   T H E   S E V E N T H   day of the party, the king, high on the wine, ordered the seven eunuchs who were his personal servants (Mehuman, Biztha, Harbona, Bigtha, Abagtha, Zethar, and Carcas) to bring him Queen Vashti resplendent in her royal crown. He wanted to show off her beauty to the guests and officials. She was extremely good-looking.

But Queen Vashti refused to come, refused the summons delivered by the eunuchs. The king lost his temper. Seething with anger over her insolence, the king called in his counselors, all experts in legal matters. It was the king's practice to consult his expert advisors. Those closest to him were Carshena, Shethar, Admatha, Tarshish, Meres, Marsena, and Memucan, the seven highest-ranking princes of Persia and Media, the inner circle with access to the king's ear. He asked them what legal recourse they had against Queen Vashti for not obeying King Xerxes' summons delivered by the eunuchs.

Memucan spoke up in the council of the king and princes: "It's not only the king Queen Vashti has insulted, it's all of us, leaders and people alike in every last one of King Xerxes' provinces. The word's going to get out: 'Did you hear the latest about Queen Vashti?

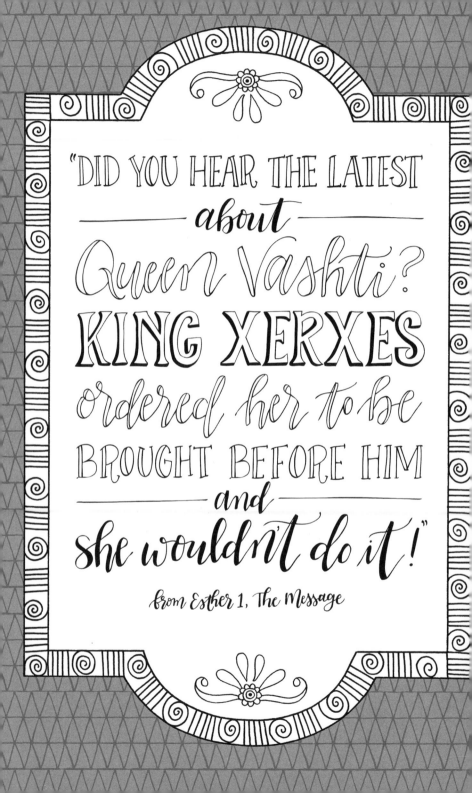

King Xerxes ordered her to be brought before him and she wouldn't do it!' When the women hear it, they'll start treating their husbands with contempt. The day the wives of the Persian and Mede officials get wind of the queen's insolence, they'll be out of control. Is that what we want, a country of angry women who don't know their place?

"So, if the king agrees, let him pronounce a royal ruling and have it recorded in the laws of the Persians and Medes so that it cannot be revoked, that Vashti is permanently banned from King Xerxes' presence. And then let the king give her royal position to a woman who knows her place. When the king's ruling becomes public knowledge throughout the kingdom, extensive as it is, every woman, regardless of her social position, will show proper respect to her husband."

The king and the princes liked this. The king did what Memucan proposed. He sent bulletins to every part of the kingdom, to each province in its own script, to each people in their own language: "Every man is master of his own house; whatever he says, goes."

ESTHER 1:10-22

6. *Queen Vashti is described as "extremely good-looking." The king seems to think so and wants to show her off. But she refuses. Why do you think this is?*

7. *Vashti's snub causes a kingdom-wide uproar. What do we learn about Susa from the reaction to Vashti's defiance?*

8. *How would you have liked to be a woman in Xerxes' kingdom? What difficulties might you have faced?*

———————— ✀ ————————

*L*ATER, WHEN KING Xerxes' anger had cooled and he was having second thoughts about what Vashti had done and what he had ordered against her, the king's young attendants stepped in and got the ball rolling: "Let's begin a search for beautiful young virgins for the king." . . .

The king liked this advice and took it.

Now there was a Jew who lived in the palace complex in Susa. His name was Mordecai the son of Jair, the son of Shimei, the son of Kish—a Benjaminite. His ancestors had been taken from Jerusalem with the exiles and carried off with King Jehoiachin of Judah by King Nebuchadnezzar of Babylon into exile. Mordecai had reared his cousin Hadassah, otherwise known as Esther, since she had no father or mother. The girl had a good figure and a beautiful face. After her parents died, Mordecai had adopted her.

When the king's order had been publicly posted, many young girls were brought to the palace complex of Susa and given over to Hegai who was overseer of the women. Esther was among them.

ESTHER 2:1-8 ———————————————

9. *Xerxes starts to have second thoughts about his treatment of Vashti, but his attendants distract him with a search for a new queen. What does this series of events indicate about Xerxes as a leader?*

10. *In verses 5 through 7 we are introduced to Mordecai, a Jewish exile, and Esther, his cousin whom he had raised. What is your initial impression of Esther?*

---------------- ✄ ----------------

H EGAI LIKED ESTHER and took a special interest in her. Right off he started her beauty treatments, ordered special food, assigned her seven personal maids from the palace, and put her and her maids in the best rooms in the harem. Esther didn't say anything about her family and racial background because Mordecai had told her not to.

Every day Mordecai strolled beside the court of the harem to find out how Esther was and get news of what she was doing. . . .

When it was Esther's turn to go to the king (Esther the daughter of Abihail the uncle of Mordecai, who had adopted her as his daughter), she asked for nothing other than what Hegai, the king's eunuch in charge of the harem, had recommended. Esther, just as she was, won the admiration of everyone who saw her.

She was taken to King Xerxes in the royal palace in the tenth month, the month of Tebeth, in the seventh year of the king's reign.

The king fell in love with Esther far more than with any of his other women or any of the other virgins—he was totally smitten by her. He placed a royal crown on her head and made her queen in place of Vashti. Then the king gave a great banquet for all his nobles and officials—"Esther's Banquet." He proclaimed a holiday for all the provinces and handed out gifts with royal generosity.

ESTHER 2:9-11, 15-18 ——————————————

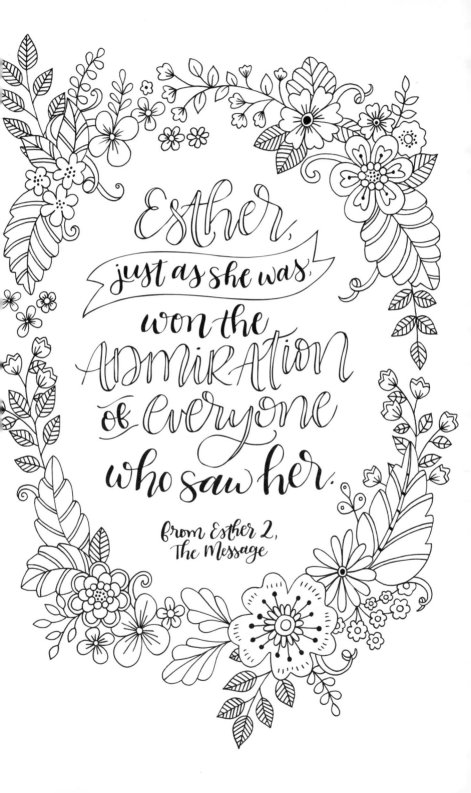

Esther, just as she was, won the ADMIRATION of everyone who saw her.

from Esther 2, The Message

11. *Esther does what Hegai tells her to (verse 15) and obeys Mordecai's instructions of what not to do (verses 9-10). Why do you think she acts this way? What would you have done in her situation?*

12. *Why would Mordecai advise Esther not to share her ethnicity or family?*

Have you ever kept secrets about your background? If so, what was the reason?

A NOTE FROM EUGENE

THE SUSA JEWS are known only from the biblical story of Esther. The elimination of detail and background leaves a kind of stark black-and-white picture of what is basic: a surviving community of faith. The community survived simply because of God's grace.

13. *Esther, "just as she was, won the admiration of everyone who saw her" (verse 15) and became queen, which brings an end to the story that began in chapter 1. Why do you think people admired her?*

14. *Where do you feel pressure to please people by not being just as you are?*

What would help you to resist that pressure to change yourself to please people?

15. *In what ways is Esther demonstrating servanthood?*

If "to be a servant is to be like God," how can you practice servanthood more consistently in your life— without giving up who you are as a person?

———————— ✀ ————————

*O*N ONE OF the occasions when the virgins were being gathered together, Mordecai was sitting at the King's Gate. All this time, Esther had kept her family background and race a secret as Mordecai had ordered; Esther still did what Mordecai told her, just as when she was being raised by him.

On this day, with Mordecai sitting at the King's Gate, Bigthana and Teresh, two of the king's eunuchs who guarded the entrance, had it in for the king and were making plans to kill King Xerxes. But Mordecai learned of the plot and told Queen Esther, who then told King Xerxes, giving credit to Mordecai. When the thing was investigated and confirmed as true, the two men were hanged on a gallows. This was all written down in a logbook kept for the king's use.

ESTHER 2:19-23 ————————————————————

16. *Chapter 2 ends with Mordecai exposing a plot to kill the king. What is your impression of Mordecai based on what we've seen of him so far?*

   In what way is Mordecai demonstrating servanthood here?

17. *God has not been mentioned in these two chapters, and yet we know he's involved—the Bible is his book! What do you think God is doing here?*

Until we meet again

REFLECT *on times you have behaved like Xerxes. Have you ever reacted badly to someone not giving you what you want, or let other people talk you out of feeling remorse for something you did? What was motivating you in your Xerxes moment?*

REFLECT *on some things you and Esther might have in common. What do you admire about her? What do you hope for her as this story continues to unfold?*

REFLECT *on some ways you can play the Godlike role of a servant this week in the lives of your friends and families, even strangers. Consider how to do so as your authentic self—not trying to be like Esther or Mordecai or anyone else.*

Prayer

Thank you, God, that though you
may not seem center stage in the drama
that surrounds me,
you are always behind the scenes,
like a good servant,
watching over me and working
all things for good.

If I Die, I Die

ESTHER 3–4

THE TIMES OF Esther were truly desperate. Genocide was about to be carried out against God's people. But even though Mordecai saw Esther as a chance for reprieve, he told her that if she didn't accept it, God would find another way to deliver his people. He confronted, but he didn't coerce.

—EUGENE

1. *Think of a time someone you cared about faced a crisis. How did you support that person? What did you say? How did he or she react to you?*

2. *Think about your own time of crisis. What did you hope would happen? What, if anything, did you say to God about it? What, if anything, did God do?*

*S*OMETIME LATER, KING Xerxes promoted Haman son of Hammedatha the Agagite, making him the highest-ranking official in the government. All the king's servants at the King's Gate used to honor him by bowing down and kneeling before Haman—that's what the king had commanded.

Except Mordecai. Mordecai wouldn't do it, wouldn't bow down and kneel. The king's servants at the King's Gate asked Mordecai about it: "Why do you cross the king's command?" Day after day they spoke to him about this but he wouldn't listen, so they went to Haman to see whether something shouldn't be done about it. Mordecai had told them that he was a Jew.

When Haman saw for himself that Mordecai didn't bow down and kneel before him, he was outraged. Meanwhile, having learned that Mordecai was a Jew, Haman hated to waste his fury on just one Jew; he looked for a way to eliminate not just Mordecai but all Jews throughout the whole kingdom of Xerxes.

ESTHER 3:1-6

3. In chapter 3 we're introduced to Haman, "the highest-ranking official in the government" (verses 1-2). Having read this chapter, what are your initial impressions of Haman?

4. Mordecai refuses to bow before Haman. We're not given a reason why. Why do you think he refused?

   Have you ever resisted pressure to conform in a situation you knew wasn't right?

HAMAN WAS FROM the tribe of Amalek, Israel's chief
A NOTE enemy during the wilderness wanderings under Moses. They
FROM were the enemy that first sought to deny Israel entry into the
EUGENE Promised Land. They came to be regarded as the opponents
of God's guidance and providence—a way of life that was
bent on eliminating not only God's people but God's rule.

5. *The rumblings and scheming among the ruling class on display here are similar to those that took place in chapter 1 after Vashti defied the king. What does this pattern of reactions seem to say about the leadership in Susa?*

6. *Haman's ego, arguably, is an extension of the culture of Susa, which rejected God as king. Reflect on instances in which power has been accompanied by arrogance. What kind of environment did the leaders in that situation create?*

How would you fare under such leadership?

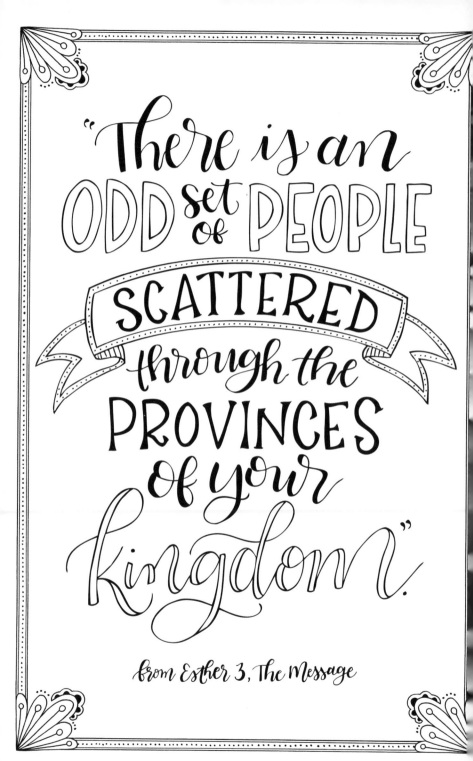

"There is an ODD set of PEOPLE SCATTERED through the PROVINCES of your kingdom."

from Esther 3, The Message

———————— ✀ ————————

AMAN THEN SPOKE with King Xerxes:
"There is an odd set of people scattered through
the provinces of your kingdom who don't fit in. Their
customs and ways are different from those of everybody
else. Worse, they disregard the king's laws. They're
an affront; the king shouldn't put up with them. If
it please the king, let orders be given that they be
destroyed. I'll pay for it myself. I'll deposit 375 tons
of silver in the royal bank to finance the operation."

The king slipped his signet ring from his hand and
gave it to Haman son of Hammedatha the Agagite,
archenemy of the Jews.

"Go ahead," the king said to Haman. "It's your
money—do whatever you want with those people."

The king's secretaries were brought in on the
thirteenth day of the first month. The orders were
written out word for word as Haman had addressed
them to the king's satraps, the governors of every
province, and the officials of every people. They were
written in the script of each province and the language
of each people in the name of King Xerxes and sealed
with the royal signet ring.

Bulletins were sent out by couriers to all the king's
provinces with orders to massacre, kill, and eliminate
all the Jews—youngsters and old men, women and
babies—on a single day, the thirteenth day of the

twelfth month, the month Adar, and to plunder their goods. Copies of the bulletin were to be posted in each province, publicly available to all peoples, to get them ready for that day.

At the king's command, the couriers took off; the order was also posted in the palace complex of Susa. The king and Haman sat back and had a drink while the city of Susa reeled from the news.

ESTHER 3:8-15 ——————————————

7. *When have you felt excluded or even persecuted for being different? When have you observed other people being treated this way? What should be our response when we or others are mistreated?*

Some people might describe Christians as "an odd set of people who don't fit in." Even the Bible seems to suggest that! What might be some good reasons to not fit in to a particular culture?

8. *Again, as in chapter 1, here we see Xerxes operating under the influence of the authorities he has surrounded himself with. Would you characterize Xerxes as a good leader or a bad leader? Why?*

9. *Haman "hated to waste his fury on just one Jew" (verses 5-6). Haman's plot is as methodical as it is brutal. In what ways does he manipulate people and circumstances to achieve his goals?*

10. *The fact that Susa is so easily and eagerly steered into acts of violence should be troubling. What does this say about the culture?*

How can we guard ourselves against participating in this kind of mob mentality?

———————— ✦ ————————

WHEN MORDECAI LEARNED what had been done, he ripped his clothes to shreds and put on sackcloth and ashes. Then he went out in the streets of the city crying out in loud and bitter cries. He came only as far as the King's Gate, for no one dressed in sackcloth was allowed to enter the King's Gate. As the king's order was posted in every province, there was loud lament among the Jews—fasting, weeping, wailing. And most of them stretched out on sackcloth and ashes.

Esther's maids and eunuchs came and told her. The queen was stunned. She sent fresh clothes to Mordecai so he could take off his sackcloth but he wouldn't accept them. Esther called for Hathach, one of the royal eunuchs whom the king had assigned to wait on her, and told him to go to Mordecai and get the full story of what was happening. So Hathach went to Mordecai in the town square in front of the King's Gate. Mordecai told him everything that had happened to him. He also told him the exact amount of money that Haman had promised to deposit in the royal bank to finance the massacre of the Jews. Mordecai also gave him a copy of the bulletin that had been posted in Susa ordering the massacre so he could show it to Esther when he reported back with instructions to go to the king and intercede and plead with him for her people.

Hathach came back and told Esther everything Mordecai had said. Esther talked it over with Hathach and then sent him back to Mordecai with this message: "Everyone who works for the king here, and even the people out in the provinces, knows that there is a single fate for every man or woman who approaches the king without being invited: death. The one exception is if the king extends his gold scepter; then he or she may live. And it's been thirty days now since I've been invited to come to the king."

ESTHER 4:1-11 ————————————————————————

11. *We switch gears in chapter 4 from the perspective of Haman and Xerxes to the perspective of Mordecai and Esther. Mordecai, and many of the city's Jews with him, engage in "loud lament." Lament is a biblical form of prayer, a kind of constructive complaint to God. Would you consider the loud lament in this chapter active or passive? Have they given up, or are they trying to make something happen?*

A NOTE
FROM
EUGENE

NO LEADER OF the Jewish community—not Moses, not Samuel, not Isaiah, not Ezekiel—was ever responsible for the survival of the community of faith. That took place in the counsels of God and by the mercy of God. Because they understood that, leaders in the community were free from the anxiety that is epidemic among today's pastors: the anxiety over survival, the worry over size, the obsession with numbers.

12. *Esther, meanwhile, is living the life of a queen. Her first response to Mordecai is to try to get him to stop his public laments. Why do you think she does this?*

When has someone else's crisis made you uncomfortable? How did you respond?

13. *Mordecai challenges Esther to "go to the king and intercede and plead with him for her people"*

(verses 4-8). But—on Mordecai's instruction, remember—Esther hasn't told anyone that she's a Jew (see 2:9-10). Not only that, but even to approach the king uninvited was punishable by death. Is Esther right to be cautious? Why or why not?

———————— ✿ ————————

WHEN HATHACH TOLD Mordecai what Esther had said, Mordecai sent her this message: "Don't think that just because you live in the king's house you're the one Jew who will get out of this alive. If you persist in staying silent at a time like this, help and deliverance will arrive for the Jews from someplace else; but you and your family will be wiped out. Who knows? Maybe you were made queen for just such a time as this."

Esther sent back her answer to Mordecai: "Go and get all the Jews living in Susa together. Fast for me. Don't eat or drink for three days, either day or night. I and my maids will fast with you. If you will do this, I'll go to the king, even though it's forbidden. If I die, I die."

Mordecai left and carried out Esther's instructions.

ESTHER 4:12-17 ————————————————

14. *Mordecai's response to Esther is famous: "Who knows? Maybe you were made queen for just such a time as this" (verses 12-14). Do you agree with this idea? Are people (or some people) "made . . . for just such a time"?*

   Have you ever felt "made . . . for just such a time"? What were the circumstances?

15. *At the same time, Mordecai assures Esther that God doesn't need her to deliver the Jews. If God doesn't need us, why do you think he uses us?*

16. *Chapter 4 ends with Esther sending Mordecai instructions for all the Jews. Mordecai does as she instructs. How is this different from their earlier interactions? What might have led Esther to feel confident to step into such a leadership role?*

17. *Four chapters in, and still no mention of God in the book of Esther. Does that surprise you? Why or why not?*

Where might you suspect God is in the book of Esther?

Until we meet again

CONSIDER *how you and your friends might stand up for people who are being mistreated in your community. Schedule at least one activity to intercede for others—maybe through a time of "loud lament," or a letter to a government official, or some other demonstration of support.*

HAVE YOU EVER FASTED—*spent a day or more going without food in order to focus your attention on something else—for some way you want God to intervene in your life or the lives of people around you (see Esther 4:15-16)? What is going on in your life or the life of someone you care about that you might want to give focused attention to? Consider a fast to help you pursue that goal.*

Prayer

Thank you, God, that you don't need us—
  that you work for our good and the good
    of those who are suffering
  even when we ignore their need or even our own need,
  or when we feel paralyzed by the need we're seeing.

But thank you, as well,
  that you choose to use us
  to love those who need love,
  to care for those who need care,
  to stand up for those who can't.

Help us to see you at work this week,
  and to accept your invitation to join you
    in your good work.

What Do You Want?

ESTHER 5–7

REALIZING THAT THERE *is* an enemy forces us to reassess our priorities. The function of Haman—or any other enemy of God—is to force a decision. The moment Haman surfaced, Esther was faced with one. What would she do? Would she speak or remain silent?

—EUGENE

1. *Have you ever had an enemy? Don't name names, but share the story. How did you become enemies? What sort of trouble did your enemy cause for you? Did you ever find resolution? How?*

   With hindsight, what, if anything, can you say was your role in the conflict?

THREE DAYS LATER Esther dressed in her royal robes and took up a position in the inner court of the palace in front of the king's throne room. The king was on his throne facing the entrance. When he noticed Queen Esther standing in the court, he was pleased to see her; the king extended the gold scepter in his hand. Esther approached and touched the tip of the scepter. The king asked, "And what's your desire, Queen Esther? What do you want? Ask and it's yours—even if it's half my kingdom!"

"If it please the king," said Esther, "let the king come with Haman to a dinner I've prepared for him."

"Get Haman at once," said the king, "so we can go to dinner with Esther."

So the king and Haman joined Esther at the dinner she had arranged. As they were drinking the wine, the king said, "Now, what is it you want? Half of my kingdom isn't too much to ask! Just ask."

Esther answered, "Here's what I want. If the king favors me and is pleased to do what I desire and ask, let the king and Haman come again tomorrow to the dinner that I will fix for them. Then I'll give a straight answer to the king's question."

ESTHER 5:1-8

2. Esther completes her fast (see 4:15-16) and prepares to see the king. Recall that the law of the land is that "every man is master of his own house; whatever he says, goes" (see 1:21-22), and that Esther has not been invited into the king's presence in thirty days (see 4:9-11). She could be killed just for daring to disturb him. If you were in Esther's place, how confident would you be that you would be well-received by Xerxes? Why?

3. Fortunately, Xerxes "was pleased to see her" (5:1-3); she wouldn't be killed for approaching the king without an invitation. Are you surprised by this warm reception from Xerxes? Why or why not?

4. *Xerxes offers Esther "half my kingdom" (verses 1-3), but she responds with a dinner invitation. Why do you think Esther makes such a modest request?*

What can we learn from how Esther approaches this tricky situation?

5. *Haman is invited to dinner as well—the first scene in which Haman and Esther are seen together. Haman doesn't know that Esther is a Jew—he doesn't know that he has made an enemy of the queen. Why does Esther invite him?*

A NOTE
FROM
EUGENE
WHEREVER THERE ARE people of God, there are enemies of God. Leadership that seeks to build up the community of faith can't afford to be naive about Haman.

6. *Beyond human enemies of God, the Bible identifies warfare on a spiritual level. When have you experienced stress, anxiety, or turmoil that might be described as a spiritual attack?*

What helps you when you feel under attack spiritually?

HAMAN LEFT THE palace that day happy, beaming. And then he saw Mordecai sitting at the King's Gate ignoring him, oblivious to him. Haman was furious with Mordecai. But he held himself in and went on home. He got his friends together with his wife Zeresh and started bragging about how much money he had, his many sons, all the times the king had honored him, and his promotion to the highest position in the government. "On top of all that," Haman continued, "Queen Esther invited me to a private dinner she gave for the king, just the three of us. And she's invited me to another one tomorrow. But I can't enjoy any of it when I see Mordecai the Jew sitting at the King's Gate."

His wife Zeresh and all his friends said, "Build a gallows seventy-five feet high. First thing in the morning speak with the king; get him to order Mordecai hanged on it. Then happily go with the king to dinner."

Haman liked that. He had the gallows built.

ESTHER 5:9-14

7. *"Haman left the palace that day happy, beaming.*
   . . . 'But I can't enjoy any of it when I see Mordecai'"
   (verses 9-13). What do you think is Haman's primary
   character flaw? How do you see it playing out in this
   story?

   When have you wrestled with someone else's opinion
   or behavior dictating your feelings?

8. *Both Haman and Esther are faced with their enemy*
   in chapter 5. How does each respond? How do you
   deal with your "enemies"?

———————— ✂ ————————

*T*HAT NIGHT THE king couldn't sleep. He ordered the record book, the day-by-day journal of events, to be brought and read to him. They came across the story there about the time that Mordecai had exposed the plot of Bigthana and Teresh—the two royal eunuchs who guarded the entrance and who had conspired to assassinate King Xerxes.

The king asked, "What great honor was given to Mordecai for this?"

"Nothing," replied the king's servants who were in attendance. "Nothing has been done for him."

The king said, "Is there anybody out in the court?"

Now Haman had just come into the outer court of the king's palace to talk to the king about hanging Mordecai on the gallows he had built for him.

The king's servants said, "Haman is out there, waiting in the court."

"Bring him in," said the king.

When Haman entered, the king said, "What would be appropriate for the man the king especially wants to honor?"

Haman thought to himself, "He must be talking about honoring me—who else?" So he answered the king, "For the man the king delights to honor, do this: Bring a royal robe that the king has worn and a horse the king has ridden, one with a royal crown on its head. Then give the robe and the horse to one of the king's most noble princes. Have him robe the man whom the king especially wants to honor; have the prince lead him on horseback through the city square, proclaiming before him, 'This is what is done for the man whom the king especially wants to honor!'"

"Go and do it," the king said to Haman. "Don't waste another minute. Take the robe and horse and do what you have proposed to Mordecai the Jew who sits at the King's Gate. Don't leave out a single detail of your plan."

ESTHER 6:1-10 ⎯⎯⎯⎯⎯⎯⎯⎯⎯⎯⎯⎯⎯⎯⎯⎯⎯⎯⎯⎯

9. *While Haman builds a gallows to hang Mordecai on (see 5:14), Xerxes spends a sleepless night reflecting on the events of his reign. Has sleeplessness ever allowed you a chance to see more clearly a situation in your life?*

10. *Why do you think Mordecai was overlooked for honor after he saved the king's life? Does it surprise you that Xerxes overlooked the chance to honor Mordecai? Does it surprise you that he makes plans now to do so? Why or why not?*

11. *Haman assumes that the king wants to honor him. What does this indicate about Haman's perspective?*

———————— ✄ ————————

So HAMAN TOOK the robe and horse; he robed Mordecai and led him through the city square, proclaiming before him, "This is what is done for the man whom the king especially wants to honor!"

Then Mordecai returned to the King's Gate, but Haman fled to his house, thoroughly mortified, hiding his face. When Haman had finished telling his wife Zeresh and all his friends everything that had happened to him, his knowledgeable friends who were there and his wife Zeresh said, "If this Mordecai is in fact a Jew, your bad luck has only begun. You don't stand a chance against him—you're as good as ruined."

While they were still talking, the king's eunuchs arrived and hurried Haman off to the dinner that Esther had prepared.

ESTHER 6:11-14 ———————————————————————

12. *Mordecai receives a great honor from the king, delivered by Haman, the person plotting his death. Have you ever experienced a reversal of fortune like this? How did you feel?*

13. *How do you think these events impacted Haman's desire to see his plan through?*

———————— ✂ ————————

S O THE KING and Haman went to dinner with Queen Esther. At this second dinner, while they were drinking wine the king again asked, "Queen Esther, what would you like? Half of my kingdom! Just ask and it's yours."

Queen Esther answered, "If I have found favor in your eyes, O King, and if it please the king, give me my life, and give my people their lives.

"We've been sold, I and my people, to be destroyed—sold to be massacred, eliminated. If we had just been sold off into slavery, I wouldn't even have brought it up; our troubles wouldn't have been worth bothering the king over."

King Xerxes exploded, "Who? Where is he? This is monstrous!"

"An enemy. An adversary. This evil Haman," said Esther.

Haman was terror-stricken before the king and queen.

The king, raging, left his wine and stalked out into the palace garden.

Haman stood there pleading with Queen Esther for his life—he could see that the king was finished with him and

that he was doomed. As the king came back from the palace garden into the banquet hall, Haman was groveling at the couch on which Esther reclined. The king roared out, "Will he even molest the queen while I'm just around the corner?"

When that word left the king's mouth, all the blood drained from Haman's face.

Harbona, one of the eunuchs attending the king, spoke up: "Look over there! There's the gallows that Haman had built for Mordecai, who saved the king's life. It's right next to Haman's house—seventy-five feet high!"

The king said, "Hang him on it!"

So Haman was hanged on the very gallows that he had built for Mordecai. And the king's hot anger cooled.

ESTHER 7:1-10 ⎯⎯⎯⎯⎯⎯⎯⎯⎯⎯⎯⎯⎯⎯⎯⎯⎯⎯⎯⎯⎯⎯⎯⎯⎯⎯⎯⎯⎯

14. *This is the second dinner Esther has hosted for Xerxes and Haman, and the third time Xerxes has promised her "half of my kingdom!" (verses 1-2). Her request is still modest—"If we had just been sold off into slavery . . . our troubles wouldn't have been worth bothering the king over" (verse 4). Why is Esther being so deferential here?*

A NOTE
FROM
EUGENE

WHEN HAMAN BEGAN to move, so did Esther. She moved from being a beauty queen to becoming a Jewish saint, from lying around leisurely to standing up courageously and speaking on behalf of God's people.

15. *Haman's fortunes turn quickly in chapter 7. Are you surprised by how suddenly Xerxes turns against him? Why or why not? What about Xerxes' character up until this point hints at this result?*

16. *Seven chapters in, and God has still not made his presence known in the story of Esther. Why do you think that is? What makes this story part of the larger story of God?*

Until we meet again

THINK ABOUT *the people you consider enemies. How can you confront their treatment of you in a constructive, just way?*

THINK ABOUT *the people who might consider you an enemy. How can you make things right with them?*

Prayer

*Thank you, God, for all the quiet
and unnoticed ways you have served me.
Help me not only to notice those ways
    but to emulate those ways as I serve others.*

How Can I Bear to Stand By?

ESTHER 8–10

JOY ISN'T A private emotion; it requires community for both its development and its expression. And since the community is provided and preserved by *God*, the response is joy *in God*.

—EUGENE

1. *When have you, or people you care about,
   experienced a kind of deliverance from trouble?
   How did you celebrate?*

2. *Where did you see God in that experience of
   deliverance? How, if at all, did you thank God?*

---

*T*HAT SAME DAY King Xerxes gave Queen Esther the estate of Haman, archenemy of the Jews. And Mordecai came before the king because Esther had explained their relationship. The king took off his signet ring, which he had taken back from Haman, and gave it to Mordecai. Esther appointed Mordecai over Haman's estate. . . .

She said, "If it please the king and he regards me with favor and thinks this is right, and if he has any affection for me at all, let an order be written that cancels the bulletins authorizing the plan of Haman son of Hammedatha the Agagite to annihilate the

Jews in all the king's provinces. How can I stand to see this catastrophe wipe out my people? How can I bear to stand by and watch the massacre of my own relatives?" . . .

The king's order authorized the Jews in every city to arm and defend themselves to the death, killing anyone who threatened them or their women and children, and confiscating for themselves anything owned by their enemies. The day set for this in all King Xerxes' provinces was the thirteenth day of the twelfth month, the month of Adar. The order was posted in public places in each province so everyone could read it, authorizing the Jews to be prepared on that day to avenge themselves on their enemies.

The couriers, fired up by the king's order, raced off on their royal horses. At the same time, the order was posted in the palace complex of Susa.

Mordecai walked out of the king's presence wearing a royal robe of violet and white, a huge gold crown, and a purple cape of fine linen. The city of Susa exploded with joy. For Jews it was all sunshine and laughter: they celebrated, they were honored. It was that way all over the country, in every province, every city when the king's bulletin was posted: the Jews took to the streets in celebration, cheering, and feasting. Not only that, but many non-Jews became Jews—now it was dangerous *not* to be a Jew!

ESTHER 8:1-2, 5-6, 11-17 ——————

3. Thanks to Esther's intercession, Haman is hanged (see 7:10) and Mordecai is given his position: "the highest-ranking official in the government" (see 3:1-2). But Esther's chief concern is for her people. Having been so modest and deferential in previous interactions, what surprises you about Esther's request in verses 3-6?

4. Mordecai doesn't revoke Haman's earlier instruction "with orders to massacre, kill, and eliminate all the Jews" (see 3:13-14); instead he "authorized the Jews in every city to arm and defend themselves" (verses 11-13). Why do you think he chose this tactic?

The order was "posted in public places in each province so everyone could read it" (verses 11-13). Given Haman's earlier instruction, how might this tactic have served to prevent violence rather than provoke it?

For Jews it was all sunshine and laughter: they CELEBRATED, they were HONORED.

from Esther 8, The Message

5. *When Mordecai is rewarded by Xerxes, "the city of Susa exploded with joy. . . . The Jews took to the streets in celebration" (verses 15-17). Why was this such a big deal to the Jews? Why was it now "dangerous not to be a Jew"?*

———————— ✄ ————————

*O*N THE THIRTEENTH day of the twelfth month, the month of Adar, the king's order came into effect. This was the very day that the enemies of the Jews had planned to overpower them, but the tables were now turned: the Jews overpowered those who hated them! The Jews had gathered in the cities throughout King Xerxes' provinces to lay hands on those who were seeking their ruin. Not one man was able to stand up against them—fear made cowards of them all. What's more, all the government officials, satraps, governors—everyone who worked for the king—actually helped the Jews because of Mordecai; they were afraid of him. Mordecai by now was a power in the palace. As Mordecai became more and more powerful, his reputation had grown in all the provinces.

So the Jews finished off all their enemies with the sword, slaughtering them right and left, and did as they pleased to those who hated them. . . .

But they took no plunder. That day, when it was all

over, the number of those killed in the palace complex was given to the king. The king told Queen Esther, "In the palace complex alone here in Susa the Jews have killed five hundred men, plus Haman's ten sons. Think of the killing that must have been done in the rest of the provinces! What else do you want? Name it and it's yours. Your wish is my command."

"If it please the king," Queen Esther responded, "give the Jews of Susa permission to extend the terms of the order another day. And have the bodies of Haman's ten sons hanged in public display on the gallows."

The king commanded it: The order was extended; the bodies of Haman's ten sons were publicly hanged.

The Jews in Susa went at it again. On the fourteenth day of Adar they killed another three hundred men in Susa. But again they took no plunder.

Meanwhile in the rest of the king's provinces, the Jews had organized and defended themselves, freeing themselves from oppression. On the thirteenth day of the month of Adar, they killed seventy-five thousand of those who hated them but did not take any plunder. The next day, the fourteenth, they took it easy and celebrated with much food and laughter. But in Susa, since the Jews had banded together on both the thirteenth and fourteenth days, they made the fifteenth their holiday for laughing and feasting.

ESTHER 9:1-5, 10-18 ——————————————

6. *The end of the book of Esther is less about Esther or Mordecai or Xerxes or Haman and more about the exiled people of God, who are now experiencing the favor of God. Is Esther's story a little story "of something that happened" (see 1:1-3), or a big story that "must never be neglected among the Jews . . . must never die out among their descendants" (9:26-28)? Or both? Explain why you think this.*

7. *The Jews of Susa killed thousands of people (9:5-19). Does the violence at the end of the book of Esther surprise you? Why or why not?*

8. *The Jews defended themselves aggressively, "but they took no plunder" (verses 10-12). Why do you think they refused to benefit materially from this violence?*

————————— ✁ —————————

ORDECAI WROTE ALL this down and sent copies to all the Jews in all King Xerxes' provinces, regardless of distance, calling for an annual celebration on the fourteenth and fifteenth days of Adar as the occasion when Jews got relief from their enemies, the month in which their sorrow turned to joy, mourning somersaulted into a holiday for parties and fun and laughter, the sending and receiving of presents and of giving gifts to the poor.

And they did it. . . .

It became a tradition for them, their children, and all future converts to remember these two days every year on the specified dates set down in the letter. These days are to be remembered and kept by every single generation, every last family, every province and city. These days of Purim must never be neglected among the Jews; the memory of them must never die out among their descendants.

ESTHER 9:20-23, 26-28 —————————————————

9. *The events in the book of Esther became the source of "an annual celebration . . . a holiday for parties and fun and laughter" (9:20-22). What contemporary celebration would you compare this Purim celebration to? Why?*

THESE DAYS of PURIM must never be NEGLECTED among the Jews; THE MEMORY of them must NEVER DIE OUT.

FROM ESTHER 9, THE MESSAGE

A NOTE
FROM
EUGENE

IS IT POSSIBLE for a community of faith to exist in a hostile world? Can a community of faith survive simply and solely because it's a community of God's people? The answer the book of Esther gives to this question is a resounding yes.

QUEEN ESTHER, THE daughter of Abihail, backed Mordecai the Jew, using her full queenly authority in this second Purim letter to endorse and ratify what he wrote. Calming and reassuring letters went out to all the Jews throughout the 127 provinces of Xerxes' kingdom to fix these days of Purim their assigned place on the calendar, dates set by Mordecai the Jew—what they had agreed to for themselves and their descendants regarding their fasting and mourning. Esther's word confirmed the tradition of Purim and was written in the book.

ESTHER 9:29-32

10. *By the end of the book, Esther is "using her full queenly authority" to lead the Jews in Susa (verses 29-32). How has Esther changed over the course of this book?*

11. *Reflect back on what you thought the message of the book of Esther might be, based solely on chapters 1–2. Now that you've read the full book, what do you think the message is?*

_____ ✂ _____

KING XERXES IMPOSED taxes from one end of his empire to the other. For the rest of it, King Xerxes' extensive accomplishments, along with a detailed account of the brilliance of Mordecai, whom the king had promoted, that's all written in *The Chronicles of the Kings of Media and Persia.*

Mordecai the Jew ranked second in command to King Xerxes. He was popular among the Jews and greatly respected by them. He worked hard for the good of his people; he cared for the peace and prosperity of his race.

ESTHER 10:1-3 _____

12. *This book is named after Esther, but Xerxes and Mordecai get the final word. Is there one hero in the book of Esther, or many? Who do you most admire in this story?*

13. *The book of Esther has one king throughout, but it's his advisors, and Haman, and Mordecai and Esther who make things happen in this story. What do we learn about power from the book of Esther?*

A NOTE
FROM
EUGENE

IN HIS RALLYING of Esther, Mordecai said, "If you persist in staying silent at a time like this, help and deliverance will arrive for the Jews from someplace else" (4:14). The words "someplace else" are one word in Hebrew. This word was most probably used here as a substitute for the divine name. For God, who is never mentioned in the book of Esther, is everywhere assumed. And like a good servant, he doesn't call attention to himself.

14. Ten chapters, and no mention of God. And yet the book of Esther is prominent in the Bible and the inspiration for an annual celebration of God's goodness. What do we learn about God from his behind-the-scenes role in this story?

15. Think about some challenges you're going through currently. Where do you suspect God might be acting behind the scenes in your story?

Until we meet again

CONSIDER *throwing a party to celebrate some specific ways God has worked in your life, or the lives of people you care about.*

Prayer

Thank you, God,
for being a good servant in our hard times,
even when you are hard to see.
Help me to see you more clearly as you work in and through my life.
Give me the boldness and the wisdom to enter whatever "just such a time" moment you might be preparing for me.

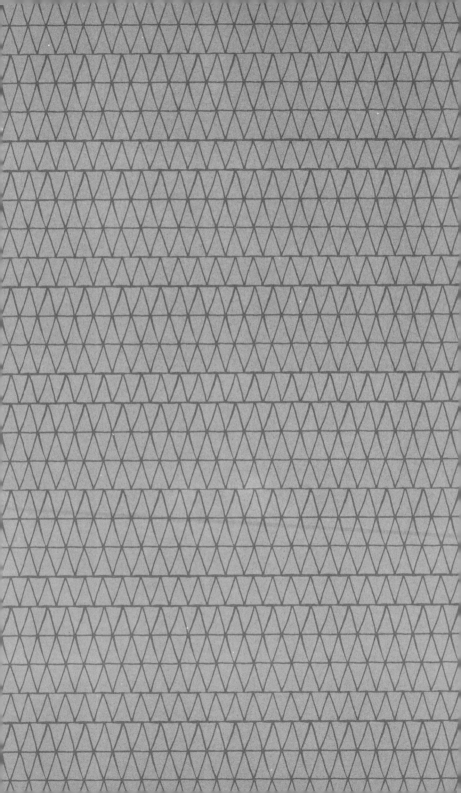

HOW TO LEAD A

Drawn in

BIBLE STUDY

THE DOMINANT AND OBVIOUS forms of Christian discourse are preaching and teaching. That is as it should be. We have a great event of salvation to announce to the world. And we have a revealed truth about God and ourselves that we need to make as plain as possible. But there are other ways of using words that are just as important, if not as conspicuous: questions and conversations, comments and ruminations, counsel and suggestion. It's a quieter use of language and mostly takes place in times and locations that aren't set apart for religious discourse. It's the quieter conversational give-and-take of relationships in which we take each other seriously, respectfully attentive to what is said to us and thoughtfully responsive in what we say in return.

Our conversations with each other are sacred. Those that take place in the parking lot after Sunday worship are as much a part of the formation of Christian character as the preaching. But conversation, as such, is much neglected today as a form of Christian discourse. If we're to be in touch with all the parts of our lives and all the dimensions of the gospel, conversation requires equal billing (although not equal authority) with preaching and teaching.

The *Drawn in* Bible Studies can be a wonderful resource for personal Bible study. But because conversation is so valuable to our spiritual growth, consider working through the *Drawn in* Bible Studies with a group. Doing these studies together can be a wonderful way of enriching each person's understanding of the Scriptures, as well as an opportunity to grow deeper in relationship. Any number of benefits come from studying the Bible together, for example:

- New insights into God's Word
- Mutual encouragement
- Prayer for one another
- More robust relationships

These Bible studies are particularly good "on-ramps" for people who are new to the Bible, the practice of group or individual Bible study, or even the Christian faith. Non-Christians and new believers can be great participants in these studies, both for their own spiritual growth and for their fresh perspectives on what can be, for seasoned Bible study participants, overly familiar territory.

These Bible studies will also be rewarding for people of all levels of spiritual maturity, offering a more reflective, creative approach to the small-group context.

As a leader, you will set the tone and manage the expectations of all participants. Not only the material you discuss but the environment you create for your group will send a message about who God is and how he relates to people. So give thought to how your meeting space can be warm and welcoming, how it can communicate compassion and care.

Because some questions invite vulnerability, and because people can be insecure about expressing their creative side, you'll want to establish and regularly reinforce the idea of grace and compassion as foundational to your group. Consider developing a "Bible study covenant" that each participant commits to, emphasizing these virtues. You'll also want to model vulnerability in how you engage the questions as they come up.

Your main job is to facilitate conversation. The study

guide is a resource to that end. The questions are designed to be read out loud. Feel free to skip or rephrase a question if it seems out of sync with the overall discussion. If your group discussion is particularly robust, feel the freedom to select only a few key questions from each chapter. Be sure to allow time and space for group members to raise their own questions about the passage you're studying.

You'll also want to manage people's expectations. Be sure to clearly establish start and finish times with as much consistency as possible. Have coloring tools on hand if people want to continue to doodle as you discuss the passage.

Your job isn't to teach, and you don't have to have a ready answer for every question that comes up. It's okay to say, "I don't know" or "Does anyone have thoughts on that question?" Still, it's good to come prepared. As you review the session before your meeting, give some thought to the people in your group—what in the passage is likely to trip them up or cause them confusion? Which questions might touch on tender spots for them? How can you be a good support for your group members as the group is meeting?

Most of all, enjoy this time with one another. You are not alone in the leadership of this group; the Holy Spirit will be moving within you and your group members. Allow yourself grace as you lead, and look for opportunities to step aside and witness the Spirit at work.

May the creativity and reflection that this guide fosters lead to good discussion and rich friendships for you and your group!

NOTES FOR SESSION ONE

Esther 1 is an introduction to Esther, but also to her context: a foreign land with a fickle leader, easily swayed by his advisors to impulsive commands with sweeping, socially disruptive consequences. Susa is not a particularly safe place to be a woman, and, as we will discover, not a particularly safe place to be a Jew.

Beyond this sense of social volatility, the book of Esther is an interesting exploration of how people in subservient roles—Mordecai the marginalized Jew who not only helps to save the Jews but saves the life of the king; Esther the powerless queen who hides her identity and risks her life merely by approaching her husband—can nevertheless have an impact on their personal situation and even on their community. The opening comment from Eugene in this session reminds us that "to be a servant is to be like God"; pay attention to how you can return to this idea as the book progresses: With God, even powerless people are never powerless; and like God, our power is best expressed through quiet acts of service. You might offer the group a "working definition" of servanthood, something like "a position that entails seeing to the well-being of someone else, usually someone with greater power or authority." Given a definition like that, the notion of a supreme and sovereign God as a servant is truly astonishing.

On a related note, we will return in each session to the observation that the book of Esther never mentions God. Some participants may find this observation especially confusing; others may find it relatively easy to dismiss. Don't settle for superficial thinking about God's apparent absence. Think of ways you can help participants connect the dots between Esther's experience and the work God is doing in their own life—even when God seems to be disengaged.

Question 4 contrasts the opening of Esther with the general thrust of the Bible: God's dealings with God's people. Participants without prior familiarity with the Bible might find this question intimidating. So try to ease people's minds as you consider this question: The point is that Esther is a unique story in a book full of stories. We may need to work a little harder to see God in the story, but God is present—and all the more remarkably so, given that the story is so far removed from the other God-stories in the Bible.

Questions 13–14 provide an opportunity for your group to discuss the pressures they feel to be someone other than who they are—to put up a front or suppress their opinions or adapt their personality to accommodate other peoples' prejudices. As we'll see, Esther grows in her confidence and assertiveness throughout the book, but right here at the beginning we see something foundational that God uses in her story: She has value just as she is. Consider as a group how you can help other people be free to be their authentic selves—whether in your local, relational networks, or related to a social concern such as human trafficking. What can you do together as a group to make your world a better place?

NOTES FOR SESSION TWO

Esther 1–2 told a relatively contained story about a king, a queen, a power struggle, and the selection of a new queen. It demonstrated that Susa was not a great place for women, but the implications of the story were pretty limited. That changes in Esther 3–4: Haman, a powerful official, feels slighted by a relatively powerless Jew (Mordecai), and sets in motion a campaign of genocide. Suddenly the stakes are raised to life-and-death.

Your participants may not be able to identify easily with genocide, but they will surely recognize that many places in the world are not safe. Point out to participants that Susa is a place where God is not honored as God. Explore the implications of that: What happens to individual people, like Haman, when they refuse to acknowledge

God? What happens to whole societies, like Susa, when people with power see no limit to their power?

Be sure to bring the conversation back to the personal level. Your participants may not be dealing personally with a genocide, but every crisis is a life-disruption, and thus causes stress and sometimes even trauma. Make sure to normalize the experience of stress and trauma (without minimizing it), and reassure people that they can safely share if and when such experiences have caused them to doubt or even reject God.

In Esther 3:8 Haman dehumanizes the Jews before Xerxes, out of his anger toward Mordecai. Consider, however, the extent to which Haman was right about God's people: To what extent does making a commitment to follow God make us "odd" to the culture around us? Is it reasonable to expect that we could elevate our loyalty to God over the people and powers around us and still "fit in"?

Question 11 might be an opportunity to introduce the practice of lament to your participants: a prayer to God that draws his attention to ways in which our world is not right. Perhaps set aside time during the session to pray prayers of lament about topics of concern to your group; this may be one way we can "guard ourselves against . . . mob mentality" (question 10).

Give special attention to the nature of Esther's instructions to Mordecai. Some participants may be unfamiliar with or uncomfortable with the idea of fasting. Offer a simple definition: abstaining from food or drink for a time to focus our prayers on a matter of significance. Some Christians broaden the practice of fasting to abstaining from media or talking or other common practices; many engage in fasts for very personal reasons (a private concern) or for relatively general purposes (as a discipline for personal spiritual growth). In this instance, the fasting Esther called for was a matter of life and death. As we'll see later in the book, the fasting gives way to feasting—a celebration of their deliverance, a vindication of their fast.

NOTES FOR SESSION THREE

It's wise to encourage participants not to name their enemies as you discuss question 1. Some participants may be recalling situations that cut close to your group, and in any case the point is to reflect on what the experience of having enemies does to our soul, and how God might grow us through the experience.

Eugene observes that Esther has moved "from being a beauty queen to becoming a Jewish saint." Draw people's attention to the changes in Esther since the beginning of the book. Take a few moments to appreciate the courage, boldness, assertiveness, and faithfulness she demonstrates when the times call for it.

This session is titled "What Do You Want?" That's a big question and can be a helpful question for people wrestling with decisions or struggling through a time of crisis. Consider putting that question to participants: As they reflect on their current life circumstances, what do they want to see happen? What do they want to ask God?

Also take a moment to contrast Esther's story—from deferential and passive to active and impactful—to Haman's story of dramatic descent from power and pridefulness to denouncement and death. Recall for participants that your study began with a reflection on servanthood; here we see the vindication of servanthood, even as we see reward for assertiveness. The two are not incompatible with one another.

NOTES FOR SESSION FOUR

Eugene's opening comment is about joy, but we still have some story to get through before we find the joy in it. Remind participants at the outset that God has been far behind the scenes throughout Esther, and yet here is Eugene attributing the community's salvation to God and rooting their joy in God. Revisit the question generally: Where do you see God in the book of Esther?

Some participants—especially those who are unfamiliar with the Bible—may be troubled by the level of violence that the story celebrates in these last chapters.

Tread carefully here: Don't be afraid to acknowledge your own unease about violence in the Bible, but acknowledge (a) the context of this ancient story is dramatically different from our own time, when such authorized violence would be roundly denounced by people of good will; (b) God's sovereign provision for his people, especially in ancient times without a moral code informed by Judeo-Christian values, remains mysterious; and (c) Esther and Mordecai put constraints on the violence they authorize that contemporaries outside the people of God (such as Haman) would never think to enact. Whenever we find violence in God's story, we can be sure there is more to the story than we easily see.

Portions of the book of Esther have not been reprinted in this study, for the sake of length. But you might consider bringing up the epilogue in Esther 9:24-26: Haman "had schemed to destroy," but his scheme boomeranged back "on his own head." This great reversal is reminiscent of the spiritual war between God and Satan: The satanic effort to see Jesus crucified, and his ministry thwarted, boomeranged back on Satan's own head, as Jesus was resurrected from the dead, thus destroying death forever. Moreover, Satan's scheme to separate human beings from God in the Garden at the beginning of the Bible boomerangs by the end of the Bible, with Satan cast down and God "making his home with men and women!" (Revelation 21:3-5).